Pola

WRITTEN BY
Jessie Hale

Published by Inhabit Education | www.inhabiteducation.com

Inhabit Education (Iqaluit), P.O. Box 2129, Iqaluit, Nunavut, X0A 1H0
(Toronto), 191 Eglinton Avenue East, Suite 301, Toronto, Ontario, M4P 1K1

Design and layout copyright © 2016 Inhabit Education · Text copyright © Inhabit Education
Photographs: © Andrew Astbury/shutterstock.com, cover · © Sergey Uryadnikov/
shutterstock.com, page 1 · © BMJ/shutterstock.com, page 2, 16, 17, 20, 22 ·
© Wolfgang Kruck/shutterstock.com, page 2 · © Dmitry Chulov/shutterstock.com,
page 2 · © Dennis W. Donohue/shutterstock.com, page 2, 7, 10 · © Nagel Photography/
shutterstock.com, page 2 · © Jarry/shutterstock.com, page 2 ·
© LauraDyer/shutterstock.com, page 3 · © La Nau de Fotografia/shutterstock.com,
page 3, 18, 19 · © Jean-Edouard Rozey/shutterstock.com, page 3 ·
© Vladimir Melnik/shutterstock.com, page 3 · © blickwinkel / Alamy Stock Photo,
page 4, 24 · © FCG/shutterstock.com, page 5 · © indukas/shutterstock.com, page 6 ·
© Kjetil Kolbjornsrud/shutterstock.com, page 8 · © Bildagentur Zoonar GmbH/
shutterstock.com, page 9 · © rck_953/shutterstock.com, page 11 · © FloridaStock/
shutterstock.com, page 12 · © Sylvie Bouchard/shutterstock.com, page 13 ·
© l i g h t p o e t/shutterstock.com, page 14 · © MVPhoto/shutterstock.com, page 15 ·
© Kasulke/shutterstock.com, page 21 · © ECOSTOCK/shutterstock.com, page 23 ·
© Christopher Meder/shutterstock.com, page 24 · © MyImages – Micha/shutterstock.com,
page 24 · © MCarter/shutterstock.com, page 24 · © Heidi Brand/shutterstock.com, page 24 ·
© Erni/shutterstock.com, page 24 · © Ronnie Howard/shutterstock.com, page 24 ·
© Tatiana Ivkovich/shutterstock.com, page 24 · © Giedriius/shutterstock.com, page 24

Printed in Canada.

ISBN: 978-1-77266-582-6

INHABIT
EDUCATION

Many different
animals live in the
Arctic.

This is a lemming.
It is small and round.

Did You Know?

Lemmings eat grass, moss, and bark.

This is a muskox.
It has long, shaggy hair.

Did You Know?

Muskoxen use their large, strong horns to keep predators away.

This is a caribou.
It eats plants from the land.

Did You Know?

Caribou travel hundreds of kilometres across the Arctic every year!

This is a raven.
It has shiny black feathers.

Did You Know?

Ravens are
very smart.
They can often
be seen playing
in the wind.

This is a polar bear.
It is the biggest bear
in the world.

Did You Know?

Polar bears are
good hunters.
They eat seals,
walruses,
and sometimes
whales.

This is an owl.
It has big yellow eyes.

Did You Know?

In the spring, male owls leap and dance to catch a female's attention!

This is a seal.
It lives near the water.

Did You Know?

A seal can stay underwater without breathing for up to 30 minutes!

This is a wolverine.
It has long claws.

Did You Know?

Wolverines have a very good sense of smell, but cannot see very well.

This is a fox.
It eats lemmings, rabbits,
eggs, and fish.

Did You Know?

Fox babies are called pups. A fox mother can have as many as 25 pups in one litter!

This is a walrus.
It has long teeth called tusks.

Did You Know?

A walrus can weigh as much as 1,800 kilograms (4,000 pounds)!

Can you think of
other animals that live
in the Arctic?